MW01093752

Master Your Mind, Mood & Attitude In The Workplace

By: Cassandra Mack

Master Your Mind, Mood & Attitude In The Workplace

A Quick & Simple Guide to Manage Your Emotions & Take Charge of Your Wellbeing At Work

Copyright © 2018, 2015 by Cassandra Mack. All rights reserved.

This book, or parts thereof, may not be reproduced in any form without the author's permission, except in the case of brief quotations embodied in critical articles or reviews. The scanning, uploading, and distribution of this book via the Internet or any other means without the permission of the publisher is illegal and punishable by law. Please purchase only authorized electronic editions, and do not participate in or encourage piracy of copyrighted materials. Your support of the author's rights is appreciated.

Published by: Strategies for Empowered Living Inc.

Disclaimer

The information contained in this book is strictly for educational and informational purposes only. Therefore, if you wish to apply ideas contained in this book, you take full responsibility for your actions. This book is solely the opinion of the author and should not take the place of therapy, professional advice, direction and/or diagnosis or treatment of any kind: medical, mental, emotional or other. This book is not intended to be a substitute for therapy, professional advice or medical advice. If expert advice or counseling is needed, services of a licensed mental health professional should be sought.

Contents

A Message From The Author

Welcome to, *Master Your Mind, Mood & Attitude In The Workplace*. I'm Cassandra Mack, CEO of *Strategies for Empowered Living Inc.* and author and publisher of this book. My company, *Strategies for Empowered Living Inc.*, is a New York based training and consulting company established in 2000 that equips individuals and organizations with tools and resources to maximize potential, build capacity and facilitate success.

For nearly two decades I have been conducting professional development seminars in the areas of: teambuilding, effective communication, leadership, managerial skills, employee retention strategies, conflict resolution and stress management in the workplace. I hold a master's degree in social work so I come to you with professional expertise in the following areas: counseling people and helping them set goals and determine their next steps for strategy implementation and alignment, understanding what drives human behavior, helping people develop life skills for personal effectiveness and victorious living as well as coaching people through milestones and transitions.

Out of my 20 plus years of professional experience coaching, counseling, consulting and designing and facilitating workshops all around the country, I developed a series of training courses designed to help organizations help their employees develop emotional agility skills and increase their wellbeing at work so that they can thrive in their roles.

Master Your Mind, Mood & Attitude In The Workplace comes out of this body of work.

Master Your Mind, Mood & Attitude In The Workplace, is an indispensable resource because when you master the way you think, respond, choose and react you develop powerful daily practices that enable you to show up for work as your best and brightest self. As a result, you become more productive and effective and you experience greater levels of success.

What This Book Is All About

Master Your Mind, Mood & Attitude In The Workplace, is a workplace wellness guide that focuses on the mental and emotional wellbeing aspects of workplace productivity and success.

Believe it or not, mental wellbeing is the single, most important attribute that you bring to the workplace. Because when your mind is healthy and your emotions are stable, you are more focused, optimistic, motivated and effective at work and in life.

There are a lot of misconceptions about what mental wellness means, so let me take a moment to clarify. Mental wellness does not necessarily mean the absence of a mental illness. Mental wellness includes the following:
- How positively you feel about yourself, the world and your life;
- Your ability to cope with change, solve problems and deal with life's challenges;
- Your ability to build relationships with others, be productive at work and contribute to the larger community;

- Your ability to focus, complete simple tasks and achieve your goals.
- The ability to respond to setbacks with resilience and respond to conflict at appropriate levels.
- Your ability to empathize with others.
- Your ability to be introspective and self-reflective in order to understand how your behavior impacts yourself and others.

Your mental wellbeing has a direct impact on your level of life satisfaction and your ability to do your job well. The way you think about yourself, your life and the people around you has a huge impact on your wellbeing. By making just a few positive changes in your outlook, attitude and conduct you can enhance your mental wellbeing. When you feel good mentally, you're able to think clearly, make better decisions, deal with setbacks without becoming self-destructive or harmful to others, be more productive and enjoy a less stressed life.

When you don't feel good mentally, your mental health tends to decline and it can become increasingly difficult to stay focused on your primary priorities and live a rewarding and balanced life.

Everyone can benefit from learning how to boost and maintain good mental wellbeing.

Master Your Mind, Mood & Attitude In The Workplace, is a resource that you can refer to time and time again, because a healthy mind requires continual self-care. As you consistently practice your new personal wellbeing and coping skills, you will enjoy the benefits of better wellbeing at work and beyond.

Why You Need This Book

Have you ever awoken on a Monday morning dreading the thought of going to work and you had to put on your game-face so that it wasn't too obvious? Be honest! If we are truthful, most of us have had days like this. However, if the majority of your Mondays start out this way, then you probably need to read this book and keep it at your desk for easy referencing.

Do you have a co-worker who is hard to get along with and it virtually kills you just to have to say good morning; even though you know good and well that you are not going to love everyone you work with? Then you probably need this book.

Are you doing all that you can to keep yourself in a good place emotionally, so that you can think clearly, make good decisions, solve problems effectively, focus on your priorities, be a team player and do your job well ...even under pressure? If not, then you probably need this book. *It's cheaper than therapy.*

Do you have a personal wellbeing plan in place to help you keep your emotions in check when dealing with difficult people and to help strengthen your resiliency skills so that you can thrive at work despite the daily annoyances and the challenges that arise during the workday? If not, then you probably need this book.

These are important questions to ask, because sometimes we think that we're managing just fine and that we've got effective tools in place to keep calm and carry on at work; until we are thrown into situations that require us to: deal with change without becoming unglued, manage competing priorities without missing important deadlines, be a team player when some of our teammates don't play nicely, shift gears quickly when the task at hand requires us to reprioritize, remain calm and level-headed when the pressure is on, deal with stressful situations without becoming distressed and work in the most proficient manner with people who we may not always enjoy working with. *But these are the very skills that are necessary in order to thrive at work.*

Not to mention, it's virtually impossible to be fully productive at work, if we don't have personal wellbeing tools in place to help us function well as human beings.

Unfortunately, many people don't connect the dots between personal wellbeing and workplace productivity. But, the two go hand in hand, because if you are stressed, distracted, disgruntled, or easily rattled, or if you're going through a tough time in your personal life without adequate support and it starts spilling over into your work, it's going to be difficult to show up for work as your best and brightest self.

Many people mistakenly believe that there's not a whole lot that they can do to get in the driver's seat of their mental and emotional wellbeing, but this is simply not true. For starters: You can develop good wellbeing habits. You can put tools in place to lessen the effects of work-related stress. You can also do your part to promote personal wellness on your job by way of your own mindset, attitude and actions.

Master Your Mind, Mood & Attitude In The Workplace, is a simple A to Z personal wellbeing pocket guide that offers 26 quick tips that you can incorporate into your personal regimen any time you need to do one or more of the following:

1.) Quickly take charge of your frame of mind and mood so that you can keep your head in a clear and productive space;

2.) Bring your most positive and productive attitude and habits to the workplace so that you can do your job well in spite of the challenges, distractions and, or difficult people who may push your buttons;

3.) Put some simple yet effective tools in place to help you: remain focused on your primary priorities, reduce your feelings of stress in the moment and keep your ultimate goals in sight.

With that said, let's begin. Each personal wellbeing tip in this book, corresponds with a letter of the alphabet so that you can remember it easily and put it into practice quickly.

I am so excited to bring this book to you. I hope that you will incorporate these tools into your overall personal wellness regimen. Happy reading.

To Your Wellbeing,

Cassandra Mack

www.StrategiesForEmpoweredLiving.com

A is for "Attitude"
Activate Your Positive Attitude

What if you could change one thing about your life that was proven to have a major positive impact on how happy and fulfilled you feel, your satisfaction and success on the job, that had a measurable effect on your personal well-being and that improved the quality of your life exponentially? Would you do it?

Can you guess what it is? I'll give you a hint: It's a mental wellbeing self-empowerment tool that each of us has complete control over. It's our **Attitude**.

When you think of a *Positive* **Attitude**, what comes to mind? Is it having your head in the clouds or being super, duper cheerful every minute of the day? Well, it's neither. Having a positive **attitude** is all about your *perspective*. It's looking at the people, things and situations in your life and choosing to take charge of your outlook by changing the way you think about these things, which in turn changes how you respond.

> A positive attitude brings optimism into your life and helps you cope with challenges.

You can begin to activate your positive **attitude** right now by choosing to redirect negative, unproductive thoughts and feelings towards healthy solutions and positive change. The stressors in our lives are either amplified or decreased by our outlook and our approach to them. With this idea in mind, make sure that your attitude is enabling you to enjoy a productive, rewarding life. Come to work with a positive attitude, by displaying a pleasant demeanor and keeping your ultimate goals in front of you.

Post-it Note

1. Consider the benefits of having a positive attitude.
2. Work on becoming more personable & flexible.
3. Develop a more positive attitude with yourself by making sure that your inner dialogue is one that empowers you.
4. Even if the idea of optimism seems farfetched, give it a try. You have nothing to lose, except a little negativity.
5. Smile more often. Be the first to say hello when you arrive at the office. Most people will be more inclined to respond positively, if you are pleasant first.

B is for "Be" Mindful
Be Mindful of Your State of Mind

Your state of mind will do one of two things for you. It will either: build you up and keep you level-headed and productive… Or, it will bring you down and undermine your success and progress. You get to decide. While most people cannot control every single solitary thought that randomly pops into their minds, we can certainly choose not to dwell on the ones that amplify negativity and stress.

Your state of mind is based on what you **believe** to be true. And the thing about **beliefs** is, your **beliefs** can quickly go from a passing thought to a firm conviction that you convince yourself is true, even if it is not accurate and not worth your time and energy. This is why it's so important to become mindful of your state of mind. This starts by evaluating the validity of your beliefs. When you evaluate the validity of a belief, you're better able to assess whether your attitude, outlook and conduct *(which are all driven by our beliefs)* is serving you well or undermining your success, wellbeing and progress.

Think of your **beliefs** as instructions that the mind sends to the brain to interpret stimuli which in turn affects your mood and drives your reactions. Your mood, attitude, actions and reactions, all stem from your **beliefs**.

> **Your beliefs are the driving force behind your actions and reactions.**

The reason why our **beliefs** impact our lives with such massive power is because beliefs determine how we behave in any given set of circumstances.

Just think about it: If you have your mind made up that everyone is out to get you, then this mindset would create a feeling in you that would determine how you interact with others. Your ability to nurture positive, supportive relationships on the job would be impacted by this particular belief.

A helpful way to figure out whether your beliefs are hindering you at work or helping you, is to evaluate your **beliefs** from time to time and try to see whether they're propelling you towards the achievement of your goals at work or are they getting in the way. And here's the critical factor: This exercise only works if you are completely honest with yourself.

Choose to start your workday by deciding in advance that you are going to show up for work with a positive frame of mind and that you are not going to allow setbacks or other people's behavior to get the best of you. Believe in yourself enough to know that you are resilient and that you have the power to stay focused on the bigger picture while you're at work.

Post-It Note

1. Train your brain to turn the tables on negative thinking by eliminating absolutist words from your vocabulary like: *Never, Always, Hate,* and *Can't.*
2. Replace absolutist words with level-headed words like: *Sometimes, Often, Rarely,* and *Can.*
3. Repeat these level-headed words over and over until they become part of your inner dialogue. This will enable you to become more flexible with respect to your belief systems.

C is for "Choose"
Choose Choices That Yield Fruitful Results

How would you respond if someone at work accused you of something you didn't do? What if you were being gossiped about by one of your co-workers or called into a meeting by your boss for something you believed was unfair? What if someone bumped into you on the subway while you were on your way to work and refused to apologize? How would you respond in each of these situations?

Productive choices are based on careful, conscious thought. Not impulse.

All day every day we get to **choose** our **choices**. Whether those **choices** are in direct response to some else's behavior, or the daily decisions that make up the fabric of our lives, or the decisive moments that significantly alter our lives, we all **choose** our **choices**. When our **choices** are conscientious; they are the product of careful thought, the weighing of potential consequences, evaluating the pro's and con's, and drawing on whatever knowledge that we have at the time.

But on the flip side, when our **choices** are impulsive and reactive; they are the result of bad habits, whim and urge. *Are you choosing your choices based on careful, conscious thought or emotional impulse and urge?* This is an important question to ask because your **choices** produce the outcomes in your life that you ultimately have to live with.

Choosing better **choices** starts by paying careful attention to how you feel in the moment as well as being 100% honest about what's motivating you to choose a particular choice. Then, connecting the dots between what you are choosing to do in that moment and how it may affect you now and later on down the line.

Today, when someone at work tests your patience or frustrates you beyond belief, before saying or doing something that could potentially jeopardize your credibility, reputation at work or employment, take a moment to think about not only whether or not the choice is worth it, but more importantly how the choice that you are about to make will impact you long term. Make sure to choose your choices wisely.

Post-It Note

1. Pay attention to the choices that you are making both big and small, especially when you're angry, bored or overwhelmed.
2. Everything from: what you eat, to what you think about, to your daily routine, to what you do with your free time, to how you handle stress, anger, boredom and, loneliness all begin with a single choice. So be mindful of your choices.
3. Recognize the difference between choices that lead to positive outcomes and choices that produce negative outcomes.

D is for "Do"
Do Something Daily That Lifts You Up

What do you enjoy **doing**? As for me, I like taking brisk walks. There's something about going for a quick walk early in the morning that clears my head and gets my creative juices flowing. I also like going to museums. No matter what you like to do; whether it's watching a sunrise, sipping on a fresh brewed cup of coffee or tea, taking a bubble bath, riding a bike, collecting memorabilia, scrapbooking, reading the sports section of the newspaper, cooking, going to the gym, painting, or something else, **do** something daily that makes your life more enjoyable. A big part of good mental health and feeling good about your life is finding activities that you enjoy, both at home and at work, and then organizing your life so that you can do more of these things.

> **Doing things that you enjoy makes your life more enjoyable.**

When you spend time **doing** things that uplift you, you give your mind, body and emotions an outlet to take off some of the stress. Plus, you increase your level of life satisfaction.

No one can define for you what you enjoy **doing**. Only you know what gets your creative juices flowing and what lifts you up. But, when you make it a point to make the most out of each day, by **doing** things that relax your mind, put a smile on your face and take you to your happy place, you reap the benefits of higher levels of life satisfaction.

Pinpointing exactly what you enjoy doing allows you to not only discover what lifts you up and centers you for the day, but it also enables you to bring greater harmony and balance to your life.

Post-It Note

1. Write down 5 or more simple things that you enjoy doing.
2. Try to do at least two things on your list every day.
3. Keep your list handy at work. Whenever things get crazy at the office and you feel like you need to release and recharge, do one thing on your list.

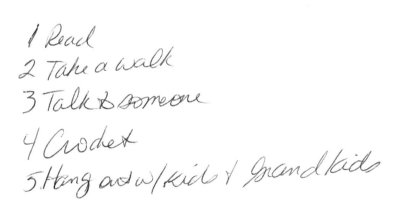

1 Read
2 Take a walk
3 Talk to someone
4 Crochet
5. Hang out w/kids & Grandkids

E is for "Energy"
Energize Your Energy

Have you ever felt so exhausted that you couldn't even muster up the **energy** to kick back and do something fun? Or like you were just going through the motions but you knew in your heart of hearts that your get up and go has gotten up and left the building? The reason you probably felt this way is because your **energy** was either low or extremely depleted. And just like a car needs gas to keep on driving, you need food, proper rest and relaxation to keep your mind sharp and your body invigorated enough to keep on keeping on.

Keep your energy level high by making better food choices, getting adequate rest, moving your body and developing a positive attitude

But sometimes between the demands at work, money pressures, the responsibilities that come with raising kids if you're a parent, managing your household, caring for an aging parent, maintaining your personal relationships, and any health issues you might have—it's amazing that any of us have any strength left, let alone the motivation to get out of bed and make the most out of each day.

Yet, **energy** is exactly what you need in order to be productive, feel good when you wake up, experience greater levels of passion and vitality, pursue your dreams with persistence and combat stress. You'll never live your life to the fullest if your **energy** is operating on empty.

The reason it's important to have healthy levels of **energy** is because when you're mentally drained, emotionally exhausted and physically tired, it becomes nearly impossible to concentrate, your patience grows shorter, you become more irritable and you're not as alert and focused as you could be. So, make sure to eat right, get proper rest and try to relax each day so that you can conserve and boost your **energy.**

Take your break at work. Step away from the computer every now and then. Get up from your desk and walk outside or around the building so that you can energize your mind and body.

Post-It Note

1. Keep your energy level high by eating high energy foods every day.
2. Don't skip breakfast. Studies show that people who eat breakfast in the morning feel more alert, and energetic than those who do not.
3. Take your break. Just like a car cannot drive endlessly without stopping for gas, you need to take your breaks during the workday so that you can have the fuel you need to work effectively

F is for "Flexibility"
Flexible Thinking Empowers You To Grow With The Flow

Ever heard the expression: *If you don't bend, you break?* Reason being is if you are not flexible, you'll have a tough time adapting to change, improvising on your strategy when what you're doing isn't working and you won't be able to quickly shift gears when necessary. In life you've got to be able grow with the flow

It's important for your own effectiveness and adaptability that you become more **flexible**. Because sometimes we can be so rigid and set in our ways, that when

> **Be flexible. Remember, if you don't bend you break.**

we encounter change, we fight tooth and nail to keep things the way that they used to be...and this can slow down your rate of progress. If you're not flexible, when changes occur on the job, you won't be able to readily adapt. Instead you'll be like a fish out of water trying to use your swimming skills on dry land when the task that is being asked of you requires you to use a different skill and think in a different way.

When you're inflexible you get easily upset by change rather than recognizing that sometimes life requires us to readjust our priorities and tackle problems in ways that are different from what we're accustomed to. When you have a rigid attitude, you end up easily frustrated and unnecessarily stressed. By learning to become more **flexible** you learn to shift gears when necessary, change your strategy when what you are doing is not the most effective strategy, open up your mind to new ideas and adjust your attitude so that you can effectively deal with what's in front of you.

Post-It Note

1. Practice becoming more flexible.
2. When you find that your attitude and methods are fixated and rigid, ask yourself this question: *Is there anything that I can do in this moment to become just a little more flexible?*
3. Try something new this week. Even something as small as trying a new dish you would not ordinarily eat enables you to practice the skill of being flexible.

G is for "Goals"
Goals Are Your GPS for Success

Each and every one of us has talents, strengths, skills and abilities that add value to the marketplace and that are beneficial to others. Most of us have only scratched the surface of what we are truly capable of achieving. And this is why having clear **goals** is important. **Goals** are your GPS for success, personally and professionally.

> **Goals are your GPS for success driving your life from where you are now to where you want to ultimately be. Goals promote greatness and growth.**

There's a theory in human psychology known as, _Maslow's Hierarchy of Needs_, which represents the needs that we as human beings have, from the most basic level to the highest level. At the most basic level are our physiological needs and at the pinnacle are our needs for self-actualization and personal growth.

So, from a human development standpoint, the journey of our lives is really about our **growth** and our **goals**. And in order to be all that you can be, you have to keep **growing** and you have to keep setting and striving for your **goals**. Always remember that if you are not **growing** and pursuing your **goals,** then you are not thriving and self-actualizing. With that said: What are some goals that you would like to accomplish this year, personally and professionally? What are your short and long-term goals? Write your goals down and allow your goals to direct your actions.

Post-it Note

1. Think about two or three things that you've always wanted to do. Set a goal to do these things.
2. Give yourself a target date and track your progress.
3. After you've accomplished a goal, make a mental note of the ways in which you have grown as a person. Don't forget to celebrate your success.

1. Read the bible by Dec 2020
2. Exercise on regular basis start Dec 2019
3. Read more - watch TV less by 3p0

H is for "Happy"
Hold On To Your Happiness

Whatever you do; never let go of the things that you do for yourself that make you **Happy**. **Happiness** is so vital to good mental health, that without it it's impossible to experience the fullness of life. Unfortunately, many people don't know how to hold on to their **happiness** because they mistakenly believe that their **happiness** is dependent upon things going their way all the time. Or that it comes from something outside of themselves like: money, status, another person, or popularity.

Despite what many people believe, **happiness** isn't something you find outside of yourself. It's a state of mind that you consciously cultivate by: choosing gratitude over ungratefulness, forgiveness over bitterness, connection over isolation, purpose over aimlessness, progress over stagnation, self-efficacy over self-pity and by focusing on the positive things that already exist in your life instead of dwelling on the negative. You have the power to increase your level of **happiness** by adopting these 5 happiness habits.

> **Happiness is not something you find. It's something you cultivate.**

1. Appreciate what you have, even if you don't have everything you want.
2. Engage in positive self-talk. Feed your mind a daily diet of uplifting, affirming thoughts.
3. Do something every day that puts a smile on your face.
4. Spend time with people who you like being around.
5. Stop putting off your **happiness**.

Post-It Note

1. If you want to hold on to your happiness, then you have to consciously cultivate happiness as a way of life; as part of your overall wellness routine.
2. Start holding on to your happy by taking charge of your thoughts, feelings, and habits.
3. Don't let anyone take your happy. No one is worth your happiness.

I is for "Intuitive" Senses
Imagination, Inspiration, Insight, Intuition and Instinct Are Your Secret Survival Weapons

Just like we have the five physical senses that enable us to navigate the physical world; we also have five internal senses that enable us to navigate our inner world with wisdom and authenticity. They are: **imagination, inspiration, insight, intuition** and **instinct.**

Imagination, Inspiration, Insight, Intuition & Instincts are internal resources that you can access at any time.

Life is filled with challenges and uncertainty. When we are faced with situations that shatter our sense of security or test our resolve, it is these internal senses that enable us to cope with life and bounce back from setbacks. Embracing the power of your internal senses is a helpful self-care practice because it empowers you to think quickly in a crisis, act decisively when your fight or flight instincts kick in and pick up the pieces of your life when adversity strikes without warning.

Just like you take care of your physical body so that it can serve you well; it's equally important to take care of your mind so that it can serve you well too. By keeping your mind as clear and positive as possible and your energy and emotions up, you're better able to powerfully engage your internal resources whenever you have to keep yourself in a clear and productive mental space, independent of the challenges you might be facing.

Post-it Note

1. Strengthen your internal senses so that they can better support you.
2. Start by finding a quiet place each day where you can take 5 minutes to clear your mind and get more in tune with that still small voice inside your head.
3. Know this: A calm and clear head cuts through the confusion and enables you to tap into your internal resources whenever you have to deal with challenges and act decisively when the pressure's on.

J is for "Join" Others
Join Your Coworkers
For Some Sort of Social Interaction

When was the last time you **joined** your coworkers for lunch or an after work gathering? One of our most basic needs as human beings is the need for socialization. From the simple *"hello, how are you?"* greeting that you say to your neighbors and co-workers, to a quick chat with a stranger in the elevator or while on line at the supermarket, to the personal conversations that we share with our family and friends, socializing is a key component to good mental health. Even if you consider yourself to be an introvert, it's still important every once in a while, to step away from your desk or computer and connect with people.

Whether you're the talker or the listener, socializing helps you feel connected instead of isolated.

The reason why it's vital to **join** your coworkers socially sometimes and try to build good working relationships with them is, connecting with coworkers prevents you from becoming isolated and alienated on the job. Plus, you never know when you're going to need a helping hand. Through networking and interacting we're able to talk to people or lend an ear when someone else needs a little support. Plus, it makes us feel connected to others and understood on the most basic human level. Make it a point to try to connect with the people you work with. Socializing reminds us that we are not alone in the world and no matter what's going on in our lives that there is somebody else who we can relate to.

Post-it Note

1. The next time your coworkers get together after work, instead of going straight home; join them.
2. Better yet, organize a gathering and invite your coworkers to join you. Even if just one person shows up, you have an opportunity to build a relationship with that individual.
3. Don't isolate yourself.
4. Participate in enjoyable social activities.
5. Instead of withdrawing, spend time with family and friends doing things that you enjoy.

K is for "Kindness"
Kindness Goes A Long Way
...So Extend It

Whenever we do something **kind** for someone else, we pay it forward. Plus, it feels good to know that you have made a difference in someone else's life, no matter how seemingly small. And here's why: On a biochemical level, it is believed that the good feeling we get when we are being kind and compassionate, is due to elevated levels of dopamine in the brain that are released when we are happy or doing something that feels intrinsically good. Our brains feel lifted, so to speak, and we get a natural high, often referred to as the *Helper's High.*

Studies show the kinder people tend to live longer, healthier lives.

Kindness can be shown in so many ways. Kindness can best be understood not as a single good deed, but as part of your overall character. The ripple effect of **kindness** is far-reaching because with **kindness** you are able to reach into a person's heart, touch their soul and inspire them to change their lives, return the favor or pay it forward. There are many benefits to being **kind** such as: increased levels of happiness, and self-esteem, feeling more mentally energized, increased feelings of purpose, self-worth and steadfastness as well as a greater sense of citizenship and community.

When you regularly express **kindness** you increase your daily diet of positive emotion, which increases your feelings of life satisfaction and overall wellbeing. Make **kindness** not only an integral aspect of your character, but also a big part of your daily routine.

Post-it Note

1. Display kindness, generosity and altruism to others, because you never know when you might need a little kindness extended to you.
2. Ask yourself: *What can I do in my own unique way to extend kindness to others?*
3. Do a random act of kindness for someone this week. It can be something as small as buying a cup of coffee for a stranger or taking off your gloves on a cold day and giving them to a homeless person on the street.

L is for "Listen"
Listen With The Goal of Understanding

On a scale of 1 to 10, how well do you listen? Be honest. If I were to ask your supervisor, your co-workers and your family and friends, how would they answer this question?

Without the ability to **listen** effectively, communication breaks down and misunderstandings occur. **Listening** is not the same as hearing. You can hear someone speaking and not be **listening** to a word that they are saying.

Listening involves paying attention, remembering what the speaker has said, seeking to understand, responding when it's your turn to talk and not interrupting. So, let me ask you again: How well do you **listen**? Do you **listen** with the goal of understanding or do you talk over people and refuse to let them get a word in edgewise?

> **When you listen with the goal of understanding you minimize misunderstandings.**

When you're a good **listener**, you learn more, retain key information, you improve your interpersonal skills and you develop better relationships because people will feel like they can talk to you and you truly listen. Today, work on improving your listening skills so that you can become a more knowledgeable person and a better communicator.

41

Post-it Note

1. Try this at home: Go to YouTube.com and watch a short _How-to video_ on any subject that you've always wanted to know more about. Listen attentively, make a mental note of what you learned.
2. When your manager gives you an important task to complete, make sure you understand what he or she is asking of you by paraphrasing the task in your own words.

M is for "Motivate"
Motivate Yourself to Put Your Best Foot Forward

Ever felt unmotivated at work and as a result you were extremely unproductive or you waited until the last minute to get started on a critical task? It's not uncommon that when we feel sluggish, overwhelmed or uninterested in a task that we may need a little push to get out of idle mode and get into success driven mode. And that extra push should always come from within, instead of your boss having to stay on top of you so that you can stay on top of your job duties. Because at the end of the day you want to get a glowing performance appraisal and position yourself for growth.

Think about it: If you were trying to get in shape and you hired a personal trainer to **motivate** you, your personal trainer could wake you up every morning, meet you at the gym, come over to your house with a whistle in hand like a drill sergeant and even call you at 5 in the morning to tell you that, "*you can do it,*" but you have to be the one get up, get out of bed and do the physical work of working out and monitoring what you eat. Ultimately, you have to **motivate** yourself to get the results that you are seeking.

> **Motivation is what gets you going and what enables you to never give up.**

Self-motivation leads to greater productivity. Keeping your motivation level high enables you to achieve your goals faster and without having to be micromanaged every minute of the day. Choosing to direct your attention on your work duties enables you to stay on task from start to completion.

In order to become a more self-motivated individual, start your day with a positive motto or mantra like: *I've got this. I was born to win. I am focused and ready for whatever comes my way today. I am a strategic thinker who keeps my word and fulfills my responsibilities effectively and efficiently.*

Also, write out your goals for the day and check off each task once it's completed. Take care of yourself physically through regular exercise, a balanced diet and sufficient rest. When you feel better physically, you're better able to remain motivated throughout the day.

Remember motivation must ultimately come from within. So, don't let lack of motivation negatively affect your performance or your performance-review. You have the wherewithal to motivate yourself and to remain focused until you get the job done.

Post-it Note

1. Pick an area of your work life where you need a little more motivation in order to get stuff done more effectively.
2. Create a list of 3 to 5 reasons why it's important for you to stay motivated in this particular area.
3. Read your list every morning (even when you don't feel like it) so that whenever you need a push to get going, you have your reasons readily available to motivate you.

Keep your joy!

N is for "No Negativity"
Keep Your Mind In The No Negativity Zone

Just like toxic chemicals are poisonous to your body, toxic thoughts, people and emotions are poisonous to your heart, mind and soul. And while it goes without saying that you cannot control other people's negative attitudes, what you absolutely can control without a doubt …is your own.

Negativity affects us in so many damaging ways. For starters, **negativity** adversely affects the nervous system, demoralizes the spirit, clouds our judgment, leaves us feeling emotionally drained, depressed or enraged. It exacerbates stress, makes us resort to toxic styles of communication like: passive-aggression, open hostility, sarcasm and its absolute worst physical aggression where we place others in danger because we are not thinking clearly. Prolonged **negativity** puts us in an emotionally unhealthy space, which can cause us to make irrational decisions rather than smart, well thought-out ones. Plus, if you are spending the majority of your time being **negative** or feeding into someone else's **negative** antics and crazy-making behavior, then you won't be able to do your job to the best of your ability and you won't have any positive energy left over to do the things that keep you balanced and bring you joy.

> **Negativity in the workplace can be managed by managing how you respond to it.**

While you cannot always eliminate negativity in the workplace – especially if it is coming from other people at work, you can minimize the adverse effects of **negativity** by first taking good care of yourself, doing things to ward off

46

stress and choosing not to allowing petty people or situations that are outside of your control take you out of character or steal the joy out of everyday living.

If you sense that someone is trying to pull you into their **negativity**, do your best not to take the bait. Try to keep a level head, even if you have to step into the bathroom to get your bearings and take a breather. If the other person is behaving immaturely, choose character over conflict by first deciding if their behavior even merits a response from you and secondly thinking about the best way to say what needs to be said, before you verbally respond or hastily send them an email. ■ Remember – *Emails leave a lasting impression that you cannot take back - even if you send out a recall email!*

Don't forget to tap into your inner resources that we discussed in section "I" of this book. Resolve that you won't let anyone or any situation cause you to respond in a way that you might later regret or that will create unnecessary stress or negative consequences for you.

Avoiding **negativity** is all about doing all that you can to keep your head in a good mental space before you even get to work and then refusing to become easily rattled by the crazy-making, unprofessional and annoying behavior of other people. Keep your mind and your emotions in the **No Negativity Zone.**

Post-it Note

1. Make the decision to refuse to let anyone pull you out of character and into their toxic storm. Find your center and keep yourself calm.
2. Although it's easier said than done; don't take any negativity from the job home with you. Commit to focusing on your goals for the day and when the work day is done ...be done with the work day.
3. Set your mind towards remaining in control of yourself emotionally, even when people try to push your buttons.
4. If you are carrying tension from the job home with you do something fun and relaxing to take off the edge.

O is for "Open"
Open Your Mind To New Ideas

Do you remember the children's classic, *Green Eggs and Ham,* by Dr. Seuss? Remember the grumpy old grouch who was extremely reluctant about trying green eggs and ham? In the Story, *Sam-I-Am* tries to get the grouch to taste some green eggs and ham. The grouch refuses many, many times, stating over and over that he does not like green eggs and ham, even though he's never tried it. Then one day, out of sheer exasperation, the grumpy old grouch finally tries it, and discovers to his surprise that he does, in fact, like green eggs and ham. There's a lesson in this story for every child and adult alike about the importance of keeping an **open mind**.

People who are **open-minded** are willing to consider a point of view other than their own. Being **open-minded** enables you to become a better problem-solver, decision-maker, team-player and strategic-planner. How? By enabling you to look at more than one way to approach a problem or situation. When you give yourself more than one option, you give yourself a variety of possible options to choose from.

> **When you keep an open mind, you open yourself up to more possibilities and greater opportunities.**

Keeping an **open mind** is good for your mental health, because it reduces black and white thinking and allows for the many shades of grey that might also need to be considered in order to choose the best possible option in any given situation. Try to remain **open** to new ideas, new possibilities and fresh new perspectives. Doing so expands your thinking.

Post-it Note

1. Talk to someone who you respect but who has a very different point of view from you. See what you can learn from them.
2. <u>Listen with the intent of learning instead of getting your point across. Try to open your mind to the other person's perspective.</u>
3. Be open to new experiences and new ways of looking at things.

P is for "Purpose"
Be Purposeful In All That You Do

Did you know that people who have meaning and **purpose** in their lives have a lower risk of Alzheimer's disease and cognitive impairment later on in life and experience more overall joy and happiness?

Further, a lack of **purpose** in life is often associated with greater stress, depression and feelings of low self-esteem. So, as you can see having a sense of **purpose** is good for your wellbeing. When you don't have a sense of **purpose** you tend to drift through life feeling aimless and stagnant. Having a **purpose** helps you to develop a vision for your life that encompasses your gifts, interests, talents, hopes, dreams as well as your personal and professional goals.

> **Having a purpose gives your life meaning and direction and it makes you a more productive person.**

In addition to having a clear sense of **purpose**, in order for your mind to stay sharp, it's also important to be **productive**. On a scale of 1 to 10 how **productive** are you? Would you say that you're extremely productive, average or minimally? This is an important question to ask yourself, because when you are being **productive** working on your important goals and tasks, you're able to clearly see the fruits of your labor in the form of a completed task or a step forward in the direction of your mission and vision. **Productivity** leads to increased feelings of success and achievement. Today, spend some time thinking about your **purpose**. Then, approach each and every day **productively** with a clear sense of **purpose**.

Post-it Note

1. Whenever you feel stuck, get busy doing something productive no matter how small.
2. Push yourself to take the first step and keep at it until the task is completed. Over time you'll begin to notice that you are becoming more purpose-driven.

Q is for "Quiet"
Quiet Your Mind

Let's try an experiment. Close your eyes for 2 minutes. During this time, try to clear your mind of all distractions and unwanted thoughts. Were you able to do this exercise for the full 2 minutes? Probably not.

Know why? Because for most of us, our minds are filled with so much clutter from the things we watch on television, the conversations we entertain, the stuff we see on social media, the information we read in our emails and just being in our own wandering thoughts that our mental space becomes cluttered and overloaded.

When you change what goes on in your inner world, you change what goes on in your outer world too.

And since our minds are cluttered, our inner clarity becomes fuzzy and hazy. As a result, we start to lose touch with our internal wisdom and authenticity - the part of our being that is clear, focused, intuitive and powerful. Believe it or not, the information that we expose ourselves to affects our frame of mind, emotions and actions.

You can choose to **quiet** your mind by doing these four things: monitoring the information that you take in, guarding your thoughts, routinely doing a mental master cleanse of your thought life and replacing negative, self-defeating thoughts with self-affirming ones. Don't underestimate the value of **quieting** your mind; so that you can mentally detox from the negativity of the day, train your brain to focus on the positive and make decisions from a place of clarity and soundness of mind.

Post-it Note

1. Recall a time when you made a decision from a place of fear, overwhelm, anger, or confusion.
2. Knowing what you now know about the importance of quieting your mind what can you do to quiet your mind for just a moment or two each day so that you can hear yourself think.
3. Instead of becoming easily distracted by all the different things that pull at your attention, try to focus your full attention on whatever task is in front of you. This is how you begin to develop the habit of staying focused.

R is for "Relax & Recharge"
Relax Your Mind & Recharge Your Spirit

When was the last time that you kicked back and relaxed? If you're long overdue for some R & R, then make it a point to do something this week that makes you feel rejuvenated from the inside out.

The reason why so many of us feel stressed and burnt out the majority of the time is because we don't know how to **relax** and **recharge**. A lot of us are all work and no play. And this is not healthy.

> **When you relax and recharge your mind, body & spirit, you reap the benefits of feeling rejuvenated from the inside out.**

There are several ways that you can **relax** and **recharge.** One way is to take 5-minute stretch breaks throughout the course of your workday. Some other ways are meditation, yoga, going for a brisk walk, getting out of the office for short breaks and getting some fresh air during the course of your workday. Also make sure to take all of your annual vacation days and sick days. You've worked for them.

Vacations are essential to **recharging** your body as well as your mental and emotional batteries. Whether you go away on a trip or you stay home and enjoy a staycation *(a vacation where you stay close to home)*, take some time to just take it easy so you can come back to work refreshed and invigorated.

Always remember that your mind, body and spirit need opportunities to **relax** and **recharge**, so that you can show up for life as your best and brightest self.

Post-it Note

1. Get up from your desk and go for a walk.
2. Take all of your vacation days and do not bring your work with you, on your vacation.
3. Bring the outside indoors. Buy a plant or a tabletop fountain, leave it on your desk and enjoy the beauty of nature at your workplace. This tip enables you to recharge your mind and emotions in the moment when you can't get away.

Know that you are where God wants you to be right now

S is for "Self-Esteem"
Supercharge Your Self-Esteem

Study after study in the area of personal achievement shows that the number one determining factor in your success is you - your belief in yourself and your willingness to self-actualize. Therefore, if you do not believe in yourself – I'm talking about wholeheartedly believing in your ability to change your life for the better and achieve the majority of your goals, then your own self-limiting beliefs can hold you back.

When you maintain healthy levels of self-esteem you are increase your overall confidence.

It's important for you to know that you are already equipped with everything you need to succeed. You were not designed for mediocrity. You were built to win. You have seeds of greatness inside of you, but it's up to you to believe in yourself and to act on your beliefs with positive conviction and then allow this inner belief in yourself to supercharge your **self-esteem.**

You may not be where you want to be right now. Perhaps you even have some obstacles to overcome or a few issues to work through, but that still doesn't negate the fact that you have seeds of greatness inside of you. So, the question for you is: What are you going to do with your greatness? Will you let you develop the necessary self-efficacy skills to live out your definition of success or will you succumb to self-doubt and never stretch yourself and strive for your goals? You get to decide! Today, make sure to make your self-esteem a top priority. Put in the work to build and maintain healthy levels of self-esteem.

Post-it Note

1. Make healthy self-esteem part of your overall wellness plan.
2. Change the narrative in your head to one that encourages and empowers you.
3. Be mindful of your inner dialogue and be more compassionate towards yourself.

T is for "Track" Your Stressors
Track What's Stressing You So That You Manage Your Stress Level

Have you ever felt tremendously stressed but couldn't quite put your finger on the exact reason why? If the answer is yes, you are not alone. This is why it's helpful to try to **track** the things that are stressing you. **Tracking** your stressors enables you to identify what's sapping your energy, recognize where the stress is coming from and come up with ways to combat it, lessen its impact or cope with it.

Here's a helpful stress tracking tip: Keep a journal for about two weeks to identify which work related situations create the most stress for you and how you typically respond. Write down your thoughts, feelings and what's happening in the moment, including the people involved, the specifics regarding the situation, the physical setting and how you reacted to it. Did you become irritable, raise your voice, talk it over with a friend or co-worker? Get a third cup of coffee, smoke a cigarette or get a snack from the vending machine?

> **When you track your stressors, you'll be better able to alleviate some of the stress in your life.**

Tracking your stressors can help you recognize unhealthy patterns, get a better handle on the things that stress you and how you typically react. Techniques such as meditation, yoga, deep breathing exercises and mindful self-talk can help reduce the negative effects of stress. Start by taking a few minutes each day to focus on a simple activity like breathing, walking or reciting positive affirmations. With practice you will find that you'll be better able to ease some of the stress in your life.

Post-it Note

1. <u>Make sure to take at least 15 minutes a day to de-stress</u>.
2. Take long relaxing baths. You can create a home spa effect by adding scented oils, candles and Epson salt.
3. Exercise daily. Whether you go for a walk, go bowling with your co-workers, take a dance class or something else, exercise helps to relieve stress.

U is for "Use" Your Mind
Use Your Mind To Calm Your Body Down

When the mind is stressed and emotions are on overload, your body will eventually react to what's going on with you internally. The danger of carrying stress physically is, if you don't release the tension, you're at greater risk for stress related aches and illnesses. One thing that you can do to help ward off the physical effects of stress is to take a quick break right where you are.

One stress relieving activity that I like involves sitting right at your desk or standing up wherever you are and focusing on each area of the body - starting from the crown of your head and working your way down to your toes. Breathe deeply and focus on releasing every bit of tension from each part of your body while bringing a sense of calm to your mind and balance to your emotions. Think about how you want to feel and focus on your desired state of being. This simple exercise will help you get rid of some of the tension that you are feeling in the moment by intentionally releasing it from your physical body.

When you learn to identify what you're feeling you are better able to release tension.

More often than not, we're not even aware of how much stress we are actually carrying in our bodies. And when we're carrying stress we tend to become more irritable, easily frustrated and less focused. By **using** your mind to release the tension from your body you become better able to ward off some of the negative effects of stress in the moment.

Post-it Note

1. Know that when your mind is stressed it will eventually affect your body. So, try to keep your frame of mind as positive as possible.
2. Get your vitamin D supply by going outside and going for a walk.
3. Try yoga. Yoga focuses on the body mind connection and it's an effective way to combat stress.
4. Strive to achieve emotional balance. Whenever you feel like you are emotionally off balance either: take a 5-minute break or do something fun to quickly pick up your mood.

V is for "Value"
Value What Matters Most

Many people never take the time to ask themselves this simple yet very important question: *What do I value most?* Clarifying what matters most to you enables you to keep your most important priorities in the forefront of your mind. Hence the popular term: Keep first things first.

Your **values** are so significant to your life that they form the foundation of your choices. So, let me ask you again: *What's really important to you?* Not what's important to your family or the people you admire and respect ...but what really matters to you?

When you look at the results of your life ask yourself: What values led to this outcome?

This is an important question to ask yourself because your **values** drive your choices and determine the direction that your life takes. Your **values** influence everything from your choices at work, to your relationships and parenting style to what you elect to do with your free time.

Often, when we are not happy and fulfilled it's usually because we are not living in alignment with our truest **values** and highest ideals. So today, take some time to make a list of what's important to you and start doing more of the things that align with your values. Whether it's spending more time with family and friends, working on creative projects, your faith, traveling or something else, when you live your life aligned with what matters most, the natural by-product is increased personal fulfillment.

Post-it Note

1. Ask yourself, "What matters most to me at this stage in my life?"
2. Write down your answer.
3. Then take daily action toward living a more value-driven life, so that you are living your life in the most authentic and fulfilling way possible.

W is for "Work"/Life Balance
Work/Life Balance Is Vital To Good Wellbeing

One of the major benefits of technology is that we can communicate with each other at any time day or night. But, the downside of technology is that it has expanded the 9-to-5 workday into the 24/7 workday, making it increasingly more complex for employees to have a semblance of a personal life. But **work/life** balance is vital to your mental health. When employees are inundated by their work lives like: being constantly emailed or telephoned about work-related issues while they are on their own time, or being asked to come in on their day off at the last minute or being expected to answer their cell phone during unpaid personal time, more and more employees feel like they are living solely for their jobs rather than their work-life being one aspect of their lives.

> Work life balance is essential to your overall well-being.

We live in a culture where it's okay for work to interrupt our personal time, but it's rarely okay for our personal lives to interrupt work. The only way to make sure that your personal stuff doesn't get in the way of work is, to make time for your personal priorities by setting boundaries around your personal time, just like you set boundaries at work.

With that said, before your answer a work-related call or email during your personal time, ask yourself: Do I really need to respond to this right now? And last but not least, take all of your time that you are entitled to by your employer. This enables you to have work/life balance.

Post-it Note

1. Don't let work take over your entire life.
2. Incorporate self-care activities into your schedule.
3. Know your limitations and set boundaries.

X is for "eXtra"
eXtra Strife In Your Life Is Like Kryptonite To Your Wellbeing

When someone is rude to you, or you get a negative gut reaction about an individual you have to interact with or you find out that somebody's been gossiping about you, it's human nature to become tense and upset. You might even feel inclined to give the individual a piece of your mind. But, if you just take 5 minutes to step back and think; you will find that 9 times out of 10 it's just not worth the **eXtra** stress and aggravation. Granted: No one wants to feel like they've been disrespected, misjudged, criticized or made to feel uneasy. And when you feel this way it can cause your emotions and your judgment to take a downhill turn. Although these feelings are completely normal and natural, there's a better way to deal than to react off of negativity and open the door to **eXtra** stress, mess and drama. You can choose to rise above the workplace drama by not reacting to it, over-personalizing it or getting caught up in it.

When you take on eXtra drama, you invite eXtra stress into your life.

Think of **eXtra** drama as a 50 lb. bag of crushed glass that someone is trying to get you to carry while you are trying to focus on your priorities. Would you willingly carry a 50 lb. bag of crushed glass? Of course not. But that's exactly what you're doing psychologically when you allow other people to pull you into their negativity. Don't open the door to **eXtra** drama, even when it's knocking real hard. Don't do it! It's just not worth your time and peace of mind.

Post-it Note

1. Remember that you don't have to let other people push your buttons. You can stay in charge of how you respond. And sometimes the best response is no response at all.
2. No matter who's doing the button pushing and trying to unload their eXtra stress, mess and drama on you, you are still in charge of how you respond.
3. Don't willingly carry someone else's emotional baggage of 50 pounds of crushed glass.

Y is for "You"
You Are Always In Charge of Your Mind, Mood & Attitude

You are always in charge of your mind, mood and attitude. No matter the situation or who's trying to get your goat, you are the common denominator in your life. You are also the common denominator in your responses to people, situations and setbacks, because at the end of the day the only person who you have complete control over is yourself. You've got to master your mind, mood and attitude so that these things don't have mastery over you. It's about keeping yourself in the wellness zone and not allowing what happens at work to take the joy out of everyday living or knock you off your game.

You have it in you to take charge of your mind, mood & attitude.

So, what this means for you is that you've got to be 100% proactive about living in a way that: builds your resilience, minimizes stress, maintains healthy boundaries, enables you to mentally and emotionally distance yourself from toxic people when you can't physically do it and make daily choices that are in line with how **you** want to feel and how **you** want to live **your** life.

You can make the decision right now to take charge of your mind, mood and attitude.

Here's a quick exercise: Envision the thought of taking charge of your mind, mood & attitude flashing across your mind like a good year blimp or a speech bubble with the slogan, *"I am in charge of my mind, mood & attitude."* Then say the words *"I am taking charge of my mind, mood & attitude."*

You are worth the practice and discipline that it takes to activate your healthiest and most productive mindset, attitude and conduct.

Post-it Note

1. Take responsibility for your personal wellbeing by taking charge of your mind, mood and attitude. Don't leave it up to your supervisor or anyone else. Because no one will ever care about your success and wellbeing more than you.

2. A helpful way to begin your journey toward better self-care and wellbeing is to make a conscious choice to proactively love yourself from the inside out. Start by thinking it, then by saying the words, *"I love myself,"* and lastly by doing things that increase your feelings of self-esteem and confidence.

Z is for "Zero" In
Zero In On Your Personal Wellbeing

Congratulations! You've made it all the way to letter **Z** which is the final wellbeing tip in this book. And it's simply this ... *Zero In On Your Personal Wellbeing* because a healthy mind, mood and attitude are vital to your happiness, peace of mind and overall success in life.

To keep yourself in the **wellness zone**, not only do you have to take care of your body, you also have to take good care of your mind.

Do your best to make choices that keep you in the **wellness zone**. Eat foods that keep you in the wellness **zone**. Think self-affirming thoughts that keep your mind in the wellness **zone**. Participate in activities that keep your emotions in the wellness **zone**. Strive for work/life balance so you can keep your quality of life in the wellness **zone**. Keep your mind, mood and attitude in the wellness **zone**, by reminding yourself often that you are in charge of your life. And being in charge of your life starts by taking charge of your frame of mind, your emotional reactions and your daily choices.

Keep your mind, body and spirit in the wellness zone.

Build and maintain relationships with positive people who help to keep you in the wellness **zone**, because they strive to keep themselves in the wellness zone. And don't forget to see your doctor for regular check-ups so that your doctor can tell you what else you can do to stay in the wellness **zone**. Be well!

Post-it Note

1. Whenever you are about to make a choice, whether it's a choice about how to respond to someone, what to do with your free time, what to eat, what kind of mood you allow yourself to sink into, what kind of thoughts you dwell on, or who you choose to spend time with, ask yourself: *Will doing this put me in the wellness **zone**?*
2. Make sure to share these tips with your manager and co-workers so that they can **zero** in on their personal wellbeing too.
3. Don't forget to see your doctor regularly, so that you can become even more proactive about keeping yourself in the wellness **zone**.

What to Do When Personal Problems Spill Over Into Work

The thing about life is this: Life never runs without a glitch sometimes. And at some point in your working life you may encounter problems that overwhelm you and disrupt your life. Most of the time you'll be able to manage the personal issues that arise in your life without them spilling over into your job. But, sometimes, when a problem becomes too difficult to handle without adequate support and, or resources it can begin to affect your work and you may need to speak with your supervisor or someone in your HR department to come up with a plan.

Even if you feel a little hesitant or embarrassed, depending on how much the issue is affecting your work, you may need to explain to your supervisor that you are experiencing some personal issues and that you are willing to get help so that you are able to do your job. Offer to make up work if necessary or ask if you can telecommute on some days. Inquire about your company's Employee Assistance Program to deal with more serious personal issues and if necessary ask for some time off if you need it.

Ask your supervisor for suggestions on how to best address the issue, and show a sincere willingness to meet your job requirements. For example, you could agree to follow an improvement plan with specific goals for you to reach, with periodic meetings or performance reviews. Do what you have to do to keep your job so that you still have an income coming in, even though you are going through a personal crisis.

Find out your company's policy on sick leave and personal days and consider if it might be time to take some time off. Find out if confidential counseling is available through your company or health insurance. Or you might prefer to seek out private counseling on your own. If your employer is offering you an opportunity to improve your job performance with a disciplinary plan, be willing to adhere to the plan and demonstrate a record of progress, so that you don't risk losing your job.

Remember no matter what problems you are facing right now, if you lose your primary source of income your problems will become worse, because on top of dealing with your initial crisis, you'll now have to deal with the problem of figuring out how you are going to pay your bills. Always keep this in mind.

In this book there's a resource section with a listing of helpful resources. At this writing the numbers and websites are current. However, if you come to a resource and the contact information is no longer current, simply do a Google search on local resources in your area that address the issue that you need assistance with.

Helpful Hotlines

Whether you're in crisis or you're looking to someone else below are some helpful hotlines and websites. Most of these hotlines are available 24 hours a day, and can help you with whatever level of assistance you need. The hotlines below are listed in alphabetical order according to topic.

➲ In any crisis, if you are in immediate danger, **CALL 911.**

AIDS
- AIDS Hotline (800) FOR-AIDS
- National AIDS Hotline (800) 342-AIDS

ALCOHOL
- Alcohol Hotline (800) 331-2900
- Al-Anon for Families of Alcoholics (800) 344-2666
- Alcohol and Drug Helpline (800) 821-4357
- Alcohol Treatment Referral Hotline (800) 252-6465
- Alcohol & Drug Abuse Hotline (800) 729-6686
- Families Anonymous (800) 736-9805

ANGER MANAGEMENT
- Anger Management Institute www.whatsgoodaboutanger.com
- Anger Management www.anger-management.com
- Inner Health Studio www.innerhealthstudio.com
- Anger Mgmt www.angermgmt.com

BEREIVEMENT & GRIEF
- Hello Grief www.hellogrief.org
- Bereaved Parents USA
  www.bereavedparentsusa.org
- Grief Watch www.griefwatch.com

CHILD ABUSE
- Child Help USA National Child Abuse Hotline (800) 422-4453
- Covenant House (800) 999-9999

CRISES AND SUICIDE
- National Hopeline Network (800) SUICIDE
- National Suicide Prevention Lifeline (800) 273-TALK (8255)
- National Youth Crisis Hotline (800) 442-HOPE (4673)

DEBT
- Debtors Anonymous: www.debtorsanonymous.org 781-453-2743

DEPRESSION
- Anxiety and Depression Association of America www.adaa.org
- Depression and Bi-Polar Support Alliance www.dbsalliance.org

DIVORCE & SEPERATION
- Divorce Care www.divorcecare.org
- Focus On The Family www.focusonthefamily.com

DISASTER DISTRESS
- Disaster Distress Helpline [24/7 hotline]

1-800-985-5990
- Disaster Assistance .Gov
  www.disasterassistance.gov

DOMESTIC VIOLENCE
- National Domestic Violence Hotline (800) 799-7233
- National US Child Abuse Hotline (800) 422-4453

Eating Disorder
- Eating Disorders Awareness and Prevention (800) 931-2237

ELDER ABUSE/ELDERLY
- Elder Abuse Hotline: 800-252-8966
- Alzheimer's Association Hotline: 800-621-0379
- National Eldercare Locator: 800-677-1116

GAMBLING
- Gamblers Anonymous
  www.gamblersanonymous.org
- GAM-Anon www.gam-anon.org

IDENTITY THEFT
- Identity Theft Resource Center 1-888-400-5530

MARRIAGE COUNSELING
- Marriage Builders www.marriagebuilders.com
- Marriage Advice www.marriageadvice.com
- Marriage Today www.marriagetoday.com

MENTAL HEALTH SERVICES
- National Alliance on Mental Illness www.nami.org 1-800-950-NAMI (6264)
- Mental Health America www.mentalhealthamerica.net
- Emotions Anonymous www.allone.com

MISSING CHILDREN
- National Hotline for Missing & Exploited Children (800) 843-5678
- Child Find of America (800) 426-5678

PARENTING/PARENTAL STRESS
- Parent Hotline: 800-840-6537
- National Safe Haven Alliance Crisis Hotline: 1-888-510-BABY

PREGNANCY
- Planned Parenthood Hotline (800) 230-PLAN (230-7526)

RAPE AND SEXUAL ASSAULT
- Rape, Abuse, and Incest National Network (RAINN) (800) 656-HOPE
- Abuse Victim Hotline (866) 662-4535

SHOPLIFTING
- Shoplifters Anonymous (800) 848-9595

STALKING
- Stalking Victims Sanctuary www.stalkingvictims.com

STRESS MANAGEMENT

- The American Institute of Stress www.stress.org
- The Stress Management Blog
  www.stressmanagementblog.com

SUBSTANCE ABUSE

- National Institute on Drug Abuse Hotline (800) 662-4357
- Cocaine Anonymous (800) 347-8998
- National Help Line for Substance Abuse (800) 262-2463

SUICIDE PREVENTION
- National Suicide Prevention Lifeline
1-800-273-TALK (8255) [24/7 hotline]
1-888-628-9454 (Spanish)
1-800-799-4889 (TTY)

Closing Words

After you've finished reading this book, you can continue to work on your mindset, mood and attitude by taking one tip each week and delving deeper into how you can incorporate that particular wellness strategy into your life.

For example: you can take the 1st wellness tip, **Activating Your Positive Attitude,** and commit to working on developing a better attitude for an entire week. The following week, you can work on the wellness tip that corresponds with the letter **B** and so on.

Continue working on each wellness tip for an entire week until you get to the letter Z. Over time you will enjoy the benefits of enhanced wellbeing.

Bring A Cassandra Mack Keynote or Workshop To Your Event or Organization

Are you an HR Director or executive facing an organizational or employee challenge within your company that needs to be addressed and explored? Cassandra Mack has helped hundreds of individuals, nonprofit organizations and government agencies develop effective ways to deal with workplace issues that impact performance and productivity. Executives, HR and Organizational Development directors have used Cassandra Mack to tackle some of the most common challenges that plague work environments, such as: ineffective or toxic communication, low team morale, workplace conflict, lack of productivity, misalignment about roles on a team, leading others towards their best success and how to coach, counsel and mentor employees for maximum productivity.

From leadership development for your executive level managers and supervisory skills for new supervisors to professionalism and personal effectiveness for your entire team; Cassandra Mack can work with your organization to help you achieve your desired results. Whether you want to maximize the diverse gifts and talents of your leaders; equip your front-line staff with the essential skills to align with vision, build team cohesion, communicate better, boost morale or adapt well to new changes, Cassandra Mack can assist you. Cassandra Mack's educational courses and professional development learning programs will help you reach your goals faster and empower your staff to do their jobs with greater skill, ease and effectiveness.

Following are 7 Benefits to bringing a Cassandra Mack Training Program to your organization:

1. Increase the collective knowledge of your entire team when they have vastly different viewpoints and work styles that hinder staff alignment and team cohesion.
2. Help your employees function better interpersonally so that managers spend less time refereeing conflicts and miscommunication and more time maximizing their team members and resources.
3. Groom future leaders for your organization. When a manager leaves the company, there is often a decline in productivity due to the company not being able to fill the position with a qualified candidate. But with targeted training now, you can help ensure your current workforce is prepared to seamlessly move up the ladder as needed.
4. Enable managers/supervisors to develop a better assessment of their employees' strengths, professional goals and developmental needs consequently maximizing employee retention and growth.
5. Better prepare your employees to develop interpersonal agility skills in order to deal with the changing demands of the workplace and business environment.
6. Align employees conduct, work habits and professional practices with the culture, mission and vision of your organization as well as the goals of each department within your company.
7. Make it easier for your organization to know where to plan, budget and allocate resources by evaluating the outcome of the training.

> ➢ For more information about Cassandra Mack's training courses go to:
> **StrategiesForEmpoweredLiving.com**

Private Coaching With Cassandra Mack

Whenever we step into a new season of life, or move into higher realms of responsibility or we want to experience greater success and effectiveness in a particular area of our lives; we must develop new tools, skills and strategies to take us where we want to go. When we have the right knowledge, the right framework, the right strategies and the right tools we become empowered to achieve our goals with greater ease and we are better prepared to step into the task that we are about to embark on with clarity confidence and competence.

The real value of being in a coaching relationship with a life coach who is bible-based is twofold: First, the Bible is the primary framework that undergirds the coaching sessions. Second the tips, tools and tactics that we will utilize together will be in alignment with your foundational beliefs and faith.

Whether you want to focus on leadership development, your relationships or your emotional well-being, coaching with Cassandra Mack will help you get unstuck, create a sustainable plan to help you achieve your desired results and provide you with strategies to move your life in the direction that you want to go in with greater clarity, confidence, and effectiveness.

What makes coaching with Cassandra Mack, exceptionally beneficial is, Cassandra bridges the psychology of success, the dynamics of human behavior, and timeless Biblical principles with her innovative empowerment strategies and 17 plus years of successful experience as an executive coach, master facilitator, social worker and thought leader to help individuals and organization build capacity and enhance wellbeing. As a result, Cassandra Mack offers her clients a deeper understanding of what's driving their behavior, what's hindering their success and how to tap their inner strengths and unrealized potential which in turn enables them to achieve their goals faster and utilize her unique techniques to make their lives better.

➤ Are you ready to live a more inspired, and intentional life? Try a coaching session with Cassandra Mack and start seizing your success and repositioning yourself for victorious living. For more information go to: **StrategiesForEmpoweredLiving.com**

Other Books By Cassandra Mack

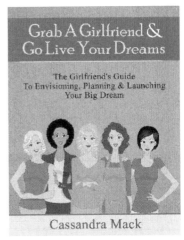

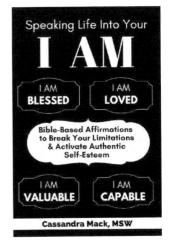

Available at: Amazon.com

54806761R00049

Made in the USA
San Bernardino,
CA